Suman Lata

A Survey On Load Balancing Appraoch In MANET

GRIN Publishing

Bibliographic information published by the German National Library:

The German National Library lists this publication in the National Bibliography; detailed bibliographic data are available on the Internet at http://dnb.dnb.de .

Imprint:

Copyright © 2010 GRIN Verlag GmbH
Print and binding: Books on Demand GmbH, Norderstedt Germany
ISBN: 978-3-656-67497-9

This book at GRIN:

http://www.grin.com/en/e-book/274572/a-survey-on-load-balancing-appraoch-in-manet

GRIN - Your knowledge has value

Since its foundation in 1998, GRIN has specialized in publishing academic texts by students, college teachers and other academics as e-book and printed book. The website www.grin.com is an ideal platform for presenting term papers, final papers, scientific essays, dissertations and specialist books.

Visit us on the internet:

http://www.grin.com/

http://www.facebook.com/grincom

http://www.twitter.com/grin_com

A Survey On Load Balancing Appraoch In MANET

Suman Lata

Department of CSE, KITM, Kurukshetra

Abstract: *The formation of ad hoc wireless networks is stimulated by the requirement of a temporary communication infrastructure for quick communication with minimal configuration among a group of heterogeneous devices. Devices used for such applications could typically be enhanced personal digital assistants (PDAs), laptops with add-on wireless interface cards, or mobile devices with high processing power. Thus, this collaborative and distributed computing environment demands interoperatibilty among the devices. The additional features never come for free as they make the routing and other services more challenging and causes vulnerabilities in network services. Resource constrained, battery powered wireless mobile nodes not only have to self configure and self monitor them but also generates a very accommodating, trustworthy and affable environment. A classification of routing protocols and their brief description, based on their operating principles and underlying features is explained in this paper.*
Keywords: *Node mobility, mobility factor, routing latency, energy consumption, network traffic*

1. INTRODUCTION:

In MANETs every node may function as a router and forward packets through routing paths. Co-operation among nodes during path discovery and packet relaying is of primary concern and should be supported for correct functioning of the network. Communication in a MANET occurs in a discrete and disperse environment with no centralized management which arises a main issue in MANET that is the breakage of link at certain moment and re-generation of link at certain state as it consists of routers which are mobile in nature i. e. are independent to roam in an arbitrary motion. A MANET is a dynamic multi-hop wireless network which is established by a group of mobile and independent nodes on a shared wireless channel by virtue of their proximity to each other. Generally low configured nodes are used in mobile adhoc networks to support mobility to user, so limited resources, dynamic network topology and link variations are the major issues with MANET. The number of link breakages observed by a node in an adhoc network can be used as a mobility metric so that each individual node can adjust its routing behavior based on the environment around it which improves the overall routing protocol performance

Requirements of Ad Hoc Networks

Ad hoc networks should give more emphasis and should also meet the following requirements to support a wide range of applications including military operations, outdoor emergencies, and natural disasters.

1. Scalability: The routing protocols employed for packet forwarding should be capable to scale for a network with a large number of nodes where the nodes keep on adding into the network dynamically. Routing should efficiently adapt itself to the network size.

2. Distributed Nature: The routing, computation and maintenance approaches in an ad Hoc wireless network should be fully distributed as a centralized approach in these domains may consume a large amount of bandwidth.

3. Communication Capabilities: The lack of any centralized support should not hinder the communication among the nodes.

4. Flexibility: Adhering to a same set of nodes to a destination throughout the routing process isn't supposed to be valuable. Freedom to select suitable nodes in terms of their reliability and computing power offers flexibility in the network.

5. Efficient Routing: The prerequisites of an efficient routing scheme are the involvement of a minimum number of nodes in route discovery and maintenance and minimum connection set up time. The multicasting of packets should make a minimum number of transmissions to all the group members.

6. Bandwidth and Resource Availability: The shared wireless link and stringent resources like transmission power, battery energy, processor power and device power must assure their maximum availability to cope up with such a dynamic environment.

7.Multifence Security Scheme: A multi-hop connectivity is provided in Manets through distributed protocols in both the network and link layers, the ultimate multifence security solution must span both layers with each layer contributing to a line of defense.

The multi-hopping behavior of MANETs is as shown in Figure 1.2 The routing information and data packets travels from one hop to another in the network, if a node A wants to send a data packet to node D, it can do so via B which is in the common range of both the nodes. However if B moves away and is beyond the range of A, the link is broken and a different route has to be established.

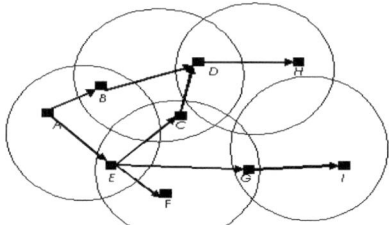

Fig 1.2 Multi-hopping behavior of nodes in Mobile Ad Hoc Networks

2. Strategies for Routing in Mobile Ad Hoc Networks (MANETs)

The most important networking operations include efficient routing and adequate network management. Based on the routing information update mechanism, ad hoc wireless network routing protocols can be classified in three major categories. These are:-

Proactive or Table driven Routing: In table driven routing protocols every node in the network maintains routing information and periodically exchange it with other nodes, which add a subsequent overhead in the network as the routing information is generally flooded in the whole network. Sequence numbers are used to distinguish recent information from the stale data. This category of routing suffers from excessive control overhead and keeps on increasing as the network scales to larger number of nodes and when the environment is highly dynamic. The nodes exchange the routing information either through incremental updates or in full dumps. Destination sequence distance vector (DSDV), wireless routing protocol (WRP) belongs to this category and offers availability of routes.

Reactive or On demand Routing: Reactive protocols obtain the necessary path to the destination only when it is required uses a connection establishment process. The routing information is propagated to the nodes only when necessary. Reactive protocols out performs proactive ones but high mobility in the network leads to degradation of performance. These protocols eliminate the need to periodically flood the network with table update packets and thus control the bandwidth requirement. The control overhead becomes low if we limit the search area for finding a path to the destination. Adhoc on Demand Distance Vector (AODV) and Dynamic Source Routing (DSR) are the quintessence of reactive routing.

Hybrid Routing : Hybrid routing supports dynamic switching between the reactive and proactive parts of the protocol and thus make use of the best features of the above two categories. By combining the best features of proactive and on demand routing scheme, hybrid routing reduces the control overhead compared to the routing request flooding mechanism employed in reactive approach and periodic flooding of routing information packets in proactive approaches. Hybrid routing sometime fails to form an optimal path to the destination node. Core Extraction Distributed Ad-hoc routing protocol (CEDAR) and Zone routing protocol (ZRP) falls under the category of hybrid routing based protocols.

Preemptive Routing: One of the efficient routing scheme is preemptive routing where an alternative path is established when the existing path is more likely to be broken by sending a warning message to the source indicating the likelihood of a disconnection which leads to an improved network connectivity. Age of the path and the signal strength are the two parameters which are adopted to compute the reliability of the links a prior. If a same set of nodes participate in the data transmission, then there are chances of these nodes failing because of their resource drain.

3. Load Imbalance: A Critical Issue

Currently, mobile ad hoc networks (MANETs) can be deployed in various scenarios but the presence of varying degree of resources, mobility of nodes and the lack of load-balancing capabilities in MANETs poses a hefty challenge for such networks to scale and perform efficiently when subjected to varying network conditions. Load imbalance is one of the most critical issues in these networks and network performance can be reached by fairly distributing load among nodes within the network. Special attention has been given to the load balancing and congestion control in network. Here it is intended to deliver data packets circumventing congested routes, so as to realize a short end to end delay and load balancing of the overall network. The various load-balancing schemes discussed offer an ability to alleviate congestion by traffic distribution of excessive load and to support better performance, taking different parameters into consideration,

4. Load Balancing in MANETs to Improve the Efficiency and Node lifetime

MANETs in its simplest sense, enable one or more mobile/autonomous entities to communicate with each other without the existence of physical connection and any established infrastructure. All nodes have to make decisions collectively. In such environments imbalance of load over the nodes can occur. The capabilities of a MANET node is a function of its resources i.e. processing capacity, battery power etc. A powerful node finishes its assigned jobs quickly and becomes idle before a less powerful node, assigned with extra work load or occupied most of the time, consuming more energy. The flow of data between the source and the destination nodes could be speed up if its efficiency split on multiple paths between them. Load balancing is certainly one of the solutions for improving the efficiency of the applications and the life of the network nodes i.e. network lifetime. The significance of an efficient load balancing technique is to minimize the difference between the overloaded and under loaded nodes in terms of their workload, keeping various other parameters in consideration. As these parameters changes in terms of number of nodes, node mobility, heterogeneity, MAC overhead and so on, the process of balancing the network becomes more complicated.

5. Purpose and Classification of Load-Balancing Protocols

The overall purpose of various load-balancing schemes is to:

- Select non-congested paths or to disseminate excessive load of a node to its neighbors,
- Balances energy consumption of the network,
- Ensure efficiency and robustness,
- Reduce end to end delay and number of packet lost by queue overflow,
- Enhance the utilization of resources,
- Improve the overall network performance and reduce collision by load distribution.

6. Need of Efficient Scheme to Balance Load in Mobile Ad Hoc Networks

Relying on a specific subset of nodes, while transferring large quantity of data causes congestion and deteriorates the whole path if, a node fails early during forwarding. Overburden some of the nodes influence not only the battery power of those partial nodes to be used up prematurely but causes high end-to-end delay. In such scenarios, a network demands an efficient load balancing scheme to be implemented so that the data flow can be reasonably distributes to several paths. A solution presented to avoid a same subset of nodes to be burdened over and over again was to use multiple paths for transmission, where secondary paths are used to transmit when the primary fails. The main purpose of load balancing is to avoid the use of specific routes to transfer data, which quickly lessen the energy of the nodes, belongs to these routes

7. Types Of Load Balancing

1. **Based on the path in which the load is Balanced:** Load balancing schemes based on the path in which the load is balanced works by selecting nodes with less number of active routes to forward data. Thus, the nodes which participate in the data forwarding and act as forwarding nodes are those having less overhead. The chances of failure of a highly active node are more than a normal node as its resources are shared on multiple routes which is a root cause of its energy depletion. This form of load balancing is not a most effective type as the energy consumption and available resources cannot be correctly determined solely on the basis of the number of routes through a node.

2. **Based on Delay:** The delay in transferring data over the path is a measure of the difference in times when the packet was transferred by the sender and the time when the receiving node receives it. Time delay measurement across a path carries valuable information with it. Firstly, it determines the length of the path, shortest paths causes lesser delays than the larger ones. The length of a path is a measure of its hops. Secondly, if an intermediate node is congested and not having enough bandwidth, it queues up the packets for processing for longer intervals and thus causes huge gaps between the packets being received at the receiver. Time delay determines the available resources i.e. the bandwidth and the processing power of the intermediate nodes. The schemes under this category balance the load by attempting to avoid nodes with high time delays.

3. **Based on Traffic:** The most effective type of load balancing is to balance the load by attempting to distribute the network traffic evenly among network nodes or paths. The term, load in a network is defined as the number of bytes of packets transmitted by the node and the number of nodes from which it is currently receiving the packets. As the node gets overloaded, excluding it out of the routes and resetting all the paths is a cumbersome task. For SD pair w, let r_w be the total packet flow rate from source to destination and split x amount of it on path p of P such that,

$$\sum_{p \in P} x = r_w,$$

This distribution of traffic among the mobile hosts fairly is useful to take full advantage of limited resources in MANET.

4. **Based on the Computed Weights of the Multiple Paths:** The weighted approaches computes the weights of the paths in terms of certain predefined parameters by computing the

values at each node. The source or destination estimates the path weight to send or receive data respectively. Thus, the path having the best metrics is selected over the others. The selection of best path must ensure congestion free, optimal and minimum overhead routing and thus minimum end to end delay. To improve the energy efficiency, paths with nodes having the sufficient energy levels are preferred. The information traverses the nodes through request/ reply packets.

Various Load Balancing Challenges in MANETs

To establish a stable balanced path which can adhere to the energy efficient and QoS requirements is a challenging issue because of the unique and inherent properties of MANETs. The issue of packet delivery system in MANET can be studied under following aspects:-

1. *Mobility Factor: The Effect of Mobile Nodes:* The communicating nodes in Mobile Ad hoc networks (MANET) are mobile or unstable in nature and form the network while they are in communication range of each other. The link between two nodes breaks, if they move out of the range of each other. Thus, this breakdown of certain links results in load balancing decisions to be made again. Hence, nodes mobility is a major challenging issue for a stable and balanced network.

2. *Energy Factor: Limited Battery Life:* The battery driven nodes of Mobile ad hoc network have limited energy resources for their own to communicate and for controlling activities. The reasons for battery power depletion are:

a.) Due to the data transmission i.e. from cluster-head to normal nodes, among ordinary nodes and nodes to gateways.
b.) Due to controlling and coordinating activities.
c.) Due to the interference from the neighboring nodes.

Thus, the depletion of energy occurs at a certain rate even if the node is not transferring packets. The energy levels of nodes greatly influence the life time of a network. If a node fails due to the complete drain of its energy, other nodes on the path becomes congested.

3. *Multiple Paths:* The existence of multiple paths between a pair of source and destination prevents the faster depletion of nodes; as if the single path is established, sending all the traffic on it consumes more energy. Also, alternate paths acts as a backup path in case primary path fails. Thus, establishing multiple paths beforehand aids not only in traffic engineering but also avoids faster network degradation. But, multiple paths for transmission add extra overhead because of the need to exchange multiple packets through multiple nodes. Moreover, the computation of the best path requires calculation to be performed at each node along the path to balance the load. Thus, distributing the traffic among multiple paths based on the measurement and prediction of network traffic incurs overhead.

4. *Node-Disjoint Paths:* The multiple paths exist between the source and the destination can either be node-disjoint or link-disjoint. The existence of a common node among more than one path, incurs much higher traffic load on this node. The node might die much earlier than rest of the nodes, which lead to the path to break down quite early. Even, link-disjoint path may have a node in common. The energy depletion rate of a specific node could be slowed down in the presence of node-disjoint paths which prolongs the network life time.

5. *Congestion on Centrally Located Nodes:* A shortest path is preferred over multiple hops route so as to minimize the end to end delay and routing latency. Traditional routing schemes mainly stressed over the formation of shortest path routing which causes the centrally located nodes to get congested. Load balancing schemes distribute the network loads, which can prevent network from getting into the state of congestion, and avoid the resources of congested node to be exhausted. The routing

algorithms in MANET that choose the shortest route to build up the communication path may incur traffic imbalanced problems in the network.

6. **An approach on Load Balancing in Clusters:**

The purpose of this approach is to find the most suitable nodes to share the load for avoiding, or at least reducing imbalances with a minimum or engendered overhead. The algorithm is invoked each time that the imbalance occurs by respecting a load threshold. The parameter for performance evaluation is in terms of work execution time and node's energy consumption. A node with high energy and low mobility will be selected as the cluster head. Mobility is the measure of a node's speed average. The load balancing algorithm here is a centralized algorithm since the global members load information of each cluster is collected by their cluster heads, which ensures load balance between its members. The cluster formation begins with finding the neighbors of each node where the distance between a node and its neighbor will be less than or equals to the transmission range of the particular node. Select the node which has the smallest value of mobility and the highest value of battery power as a cluster head and designate all its neighbors as its members. After reaching a minimum threshold of energy, cluster head again invokes the election procedure. When the network is set up each node sends a HELLO message to diffuse its ID, which is recorded by all of its neighbor nodes. As the load balancing algorithm is implemented at the level of each cluster, the maintenance of load balancing in each cluster is the principal role of a cluster head. It collects   information about each member node such as energy and load values periodically.

Two thresholds, for the maximum load that a node is able to carry and the minimum energy, are defined for each node. If a node detects any or both the thresholds to be reached then it generates a Discharge Request for the respective cluster head, which consults its member table to find a node with highest energy and smallest load. If a node is found, send a response message to the requesting node indicating the address of the new node that will receive the extra load. The requesting node will select a new node on the basis of its distance from it, if a cluster head send more than one addresses. The transfer of load over a smaller distance will incur lower transfer cost than transfer over longer paths. When an overloaded node transfers its load to other new nodes frequently, then it will spend more time on sending of load than on its processing. This can be minimized by changing the route or excluding that congested node from the route to avoid thrashing activity.

7. **Conclusion & Future Scope:**

First the adhoc networks are more vulnerable to security attacks due to the lack of limited physical protection of broadcast medium. In such scenarios **Authentication** is one of the most remarkable security aspects in any system because all the remaining attributes depends completely on it. Secondly, efficient resource usage and   utilization of the available limited amount of energy in deploying the network in the most efficient way is one of the greatest challenges faced by adhoc networks. The network performance might be improved if the network is clustered more proficiently by grouping together nodes that are in close proximity via efficient **Clustering** scheme. Thirdly, the radio links in MANETs are opportunistic because of the restricted bandwidth between the nodes thus **Load balancing** is of vital importance in such networks. Due to inherent properties of MANETs, providing a robust solution these issues is a challenging task.

Refrences:

[1]   Loay Abusalah, Ashfaq Khokhar and Mohsen Guizani, " A Survey of Secure Mobile
        Ad Hoc Routing Protocols", 1553-877X/08/IEEE 2008.
[2]   Kavitha Ammayappan, V.N.Sastry and Atul Negi, "Cluster based Multihop Security
        Protocol in MANET using ECC", 2007 IEEE
[3]   Todd R. Andel, Alec Yasinsac, "Adaptive Threat Modeling for Secure Ad Hoc
        Routing Protocols" Electronic Notes in Theoretical Computer Science 197 (2008) 3–
        14 1571-0661 © 2008 Elsevier B.V. doi:10.1016/j.entcs.2007.12.013
[4]   Genevieve Arboit, Claude Cre peau, Carlton R. Davis, Muthucumaru   Maheswaran,
        "A localized certificate revocation scheme for mobile ad hoc networks" Ad Hoc
        Networks   6   (2008)   17–31   1570-8705   2006   Elsevier   B.V.
        doi:10.1016/j.adhoc.2006.07.003
[5]   Daniel Augot, Raghav Bhaskar, Valerie Issarnyb, Daniele Sacchetti, "A three round
        authenticated group key agreement protocol for ad hoc networks" Pervasive and
        Mobile Computing 3 (2007) 36–52 1574-1192 2006 Elsevier B.V.
        doi:10.1016/j.pmcj.2006.07.001
[6]   E. Ayday, F. Fekri, "A protocol for data availability in Mobile Ad-Hoc Networks in
        the presence of insider attacks" Ad Hoc Networks 8 (2010) 181–192 1570-8705
        Published by Elsevier B.V.doi:10.1016/j.adhoc.2009.07.001
[7]   Angelo Bannack, Luiz Carlos Pessoa Albini, "Investigating the Load Balance of
        Multipath Routing to Increase the Lifetime of a MANET", ©2008 IEEE.
[8]   Muhammad Bohio, Ali Miri, "Efficient identity-based security schemes for ad hoc
        network routing protocols" Ad Hoc Networks 2 (2004) 309–317 1570-8705 2004
        Elsevier B.V. doi:10.1016/j.adhoc.2004.03.011 [Cas,07]Claude Castelluccia, Nitesh
        Saxena, Jeong Hyun Yi, "Robust self-keying mobile ad hoc networks" Computer
[9]   Networks 51 (2007) 1169–1182 1389-1286 2006 Elsevier B.V.
        doi:10.1016/j.comnet.2006.07.009
[10]   S.Buchegger and J.L. Boudec, "Performance Analysis of the Confident Protocol in
        dynamic Ad Hoc Networks IEEE/ACM Symp., 2002
[11]   Bogdan Carbunar, Ioanis Ioannidis and Cristina Nita-Rotaru, "JANUS: Towards
        Robust and Malicious Resilient Routing in Hybrid Wireless Networks" WiSe'04,
        October 1, 2004, Philadelphia, Pennsylvania, USA. Copyright 2004 ACM 1-58113-
        925-X/04/0010
[12]   Claude Castelluccia, Nitesh Saxena, Jeong Hyun Yi, "Robust self-keying mobile ad
        hoc networks" Computer Networks 51 (2007) 1169–1182 1389-1286 2006 Elsevier
        B.V. doi:10.1016/j.comnet.2006.07.009
[13]   Gautam Chakrabarti, Sandeep Kulkarni, "Load balancing and resource reservation in
        mobile ad hoc networks" Ad Hoc Networks 4 (2006) 186–203 1570-8705 2004
        Elsevier B.V. doi:10.1016/j.adhoc.2004.04.012
[14]   Xiaoqin Chen, Harley M. Jones, A.D.S. Jayalath: Congestion-Aware Routing
        Protocol for Mobile Ad Hoc Networks, 1-4244-0264-6/07 ©2010 IEEE.
[15]   Yang Clin, Y. Y. Wen, "A Routing Protocol with Energy and Traffic Balance
        Awareness in Wireless Ad hoc Networks", 2007 IEEE.